WASHINGTON

The Evergreen State

BY
JOHN HAMILTON

Abdo & Daughters
An imprint of Abdo Publishing | abdopublishing.com

abdopublishing.com

Published by ABDO Publishing, a division of ABDO, PO Box 398166, Minneapolis, Minnesota 55439. Copyright © 2017 by Abdo Consulting Group, Inc. International copyrights reserved in all countries. No part of this book may be reproduced in any form without written permission from the publisher. ABDO & Daughters™ is a trademark and logo of ABDO Publishing.

Printed in the United States of America, North Mankato, Minnesota.
072016
092016

THIS BOOK CONTAINS
RECYCLED MATERIALS

Editor: Sue Hamilton   **Contributing Editor:** Bridget O'Brien
Graphic Design: Sue Hamilton
Cover Art Direction: Candice Keimig   **Cover Photo Selection:** Neil Klinepier
Cover Photo: iStock
Interior Images: Alamy, Amtrak, AP, Boeing, City of Tumwater/R. Schlect, Dr. Macro, Eastern Washington University, Edward Curtis, Getty, Granger, History in Full Color-Restoration/Colorization, Independence National Historical Park/C.W. Peale, iStock, Jacobolus, James G. Swan, Library of Congress, Living in Olympia, Mile High Maps, Minden Pictures, Mountain High Flags, National Portrait Gallery-London, One Mile Up, Seattle Mariners, Seattle Seahawks, Seattle Sounders, Seattle Storm, Seattle University, Secretary of State-Washington State, U.S. Geological Survey, University of Washington Libraries, Wikimedia, and Woodland Park Zoo.

Statistics: *State and City Populations*, U.S. Census Bureau, July 1, 2015 estimates; *Land and Water Area*, U.S. Census Bureau, 2010 Census, MAF/TIGER database; *State Temperature Extremes*, NOAA National Climatic Data Center; *Climatology and Average Annual Precipitation*, NOAA National Climatic Data Center, 1980-2015 statewide averages; *State Highest and Lowest Points*, NOAA National Geodetic Survey.

Websites: To learn more about the United States, visit booklinks.abdopublishing.com. These links are routinely monitored and updated to provide the most current information available.

Cataloging-in-Publication Data
Names: Hamilton, John, 1959- author.
Title: Washington / by John Hamilton.
Description: Minneapolis, MN : Abdo Publishing, [2017] | Series: The United
    States of America | Includes index.
Identifiers: LCCN 2015957745 | ISBN 9781680783506 (lib. bdg.) |
    ISBN 9781680774542 (ebook)
Subjects: LCSH: Washington (State)--Juvenile literature.
Classification: DDC 979.7--dc23
LC record available at http://lccn.loc.gov/2015957745

CONTENTS

THE EVERGREEN STATE

Washington is named after George Washington, the nation's first president. It is the only state named after a United States president. Some people confuse it for the nation's capital, Washington, DC. For that reason, Washington is often called "the state of Washington," or "Washington state."

More than half of Washington's citizens live in the bustling Seattle area. There is plenty to do in the big city (including taking a breathtaking ride on the Space Needle), but Washingtonians are nature lovers. They love filling their lungs with fresh mountain air, or strolling across miles of beaches along the Pacific Ocean coast.

Seattle's famous Space Needle stands 605 feet (184 m) tall.

Much of Washington is heavily forested, especially west of the Cascade Range. There are dense woods filled with evergreen trees such as Douglas fir and ponderosa pine. Frequent rainfall helps foliage grow on the forest floor, even in the drier summer months. That is why Washington is nicknamed "The Evergreen State."

QUICK FACTS

Name: Washington is named after George Washington, the first president of the United States.

State Capital: Olympia, population 50,302

Date of Statehood: November 11, 1889 (42nd state)

Population: 7,170,351 (13th-most populous state)

Area (Total Land and Water): 71,298 square miles (184,661 sq km), 18th-largest state

Largest City: Seattle, population 684,451

Nickname: The Evergreen State

Motto: *Alki* (Into the Future/By and By)

State Bird: Willow Goldfinch

State Flower: Coast Rhododendron

State Gem: Petrified Wood

State Tree: Western Hemlock

State Song: "Washington, My Home"

Highest Point: Mount Rainier, 14,411 feet (4,392 m)

Lowest Point: Pacific Ocean, 0 feet (0 m)

Average July High Temperature: 78°F (26°C)

Record High Temperature: 118°F (48°C), at Ice Harbor Dam, near Pasco, on August 5, 1961

Average January Low Temperature: 26°F (-3°C)

Record Low Temperature: -48°F (-44°C), in Mazama on December 30, 1968

Average Annual Precipitation: Varies greatly across the state. 109 inches (277 cm) in the West Olympic Coast region; 8 inches (20 cm) in the Yakima area.

Number of U.S. Senators: 2

Number of U.S. Representatives: 10

U.S. Postal Service Abbreviation: WA

GEOGRAPHY

Washington is in the Pacific Northwest region of the United States. It covers 71,298 square miles (184,661 sq km) of land and water. That makes it the 18th-largest state. It shares borders with Oregon to the south, Idaho to the east, and the nation of Canada to the north. To the west is the Pacific Ocean.

Washington's western side is rainy and filled with dense forests. Millions of people live along the Pacific Ocean coast. Washington's eastern side is more arid, flat, and less populated. The Cascade Range is a series of towering peaks that run north and south across the middle of the state. Mount Rainier soars to 14,411 feet (4,392 m). Its summit is the tallest point in Washington. There are glaciers on many of the highest mountains. The Cascade Range also includes several volcanic peaks. Southern Washington's Mount St. Helens blew its top on May 18, 1980. The eruption killed dozens of people and caused much damage.

Mount St. Helens

Washington's total land and water area is 71,298 square miles (184,661 sq km). It is the 18th-largest state. The state capital is Olympia.

The western side of Washington meets the Pacific Ocean. Along the coast, there are stretches of flat land suitable for large cities. About half of Washington's population lives in the Seattle area.

In the northwest is a long, deep ocean inlet called Puget Sound. It is nearly 100 miles (161 km) long. Its deep waters make Seattle a good harbor for ships. Other major cities along the sound include Everett, Tacoma, and Washington's capital of Olympia.

In the far northwestern corner of the state is the Olympic Peninsula. There are dense woodlands, including rain forests. The rugged Pacific Ocean coast is to the west. The Olympic Mountains dominate the center of the peninsula. To the north is the Strait of Juan de Fuca, which is home to migrating whales, including orcas.

Washington's rugged Pacific Ocean coast.

When rain clouds blow eastward from the Pacific Ocean, they must rise to pass over the tall mountains of the Cascade Range. Their moisture condenses and falls as rain or snow. By the time the clouds blow over the mountains, they have little moisture left. This "rain shadow" effect is why eastern Washington receives much less rain than the rest of the state.

Much of southeastern Washington is a semi-arid region called the Columbia Plateau. It is covered in grasslands. There are some mountains, such as the forested Blue Mountains in the southeastern corner of the state. The gently rolling hills of the Palouse region have been converted to farmland, where fields of wheat are grown.

Major rivers in Washington include the Columbia, Snake, and Yakima Rivers. The largest natural lakes include Lake Chelan and Lake Washington.

CLIMATE AND WEATHER

The warm waters of the Pacific Ocean cause the western side of Washington to have a mild, damp climate. Compared to most states in the middle of North America, summers in the Pacific Northwest region are cooler, and winters are warmer. In Seattle, the average July temperature is just 66°F (19°C). In January, the average is 42°F (6°C).

The record high temperature in Washington is 118°F (48°C). It occurred at Ice Harbor Dam, near the city of Pasco, on August 5, 1961. The record low occurred in the mountainous town of Mazama, near North Cascades National Park, on December 30, 1968. On that day, the thermometer plunged to -48°F (-44°C).

Seattle receives about 155 days of measurable rain per year. Coastal Washington state is among the wettest places on the West Coast.

A ferry sails into Seattle through a fog bank. The city averages 226 days of heavy cloud cover each year. That is the most of any major United States city.

Along the coast, and on the western side of the Cascade Range, there is a lot of rain. Some areas annually receive as much as 100 inches (254 cm) of precipitation or more. The tall mountains act like a wall that stops moist, mild air blowing in from the Pacific Ocean. On the east side of the mountains, there is much less rain.

CLIMATE AND WEATHER

PLANTS AND
ANIMALS

About 22 million acres (8.9 million ha) of Washington is forestland, which covers nearly half the state. Most of the forests are west of the mountains of the Cascade Range. Some are also in the northeastern corner of the state, and the extreme southeast.

Washington's forests are dominated by evergreen trees. In the rainy Olympic Peninsula coast are forests of Sitka spruce and western hemlock. Farther inland are Douglas fir, western hemlock, ponderosa pine, and western red cedar. There are also deciduous trees such as maple and aspen. Washington's official state tree is the western hemlock.

A Roosevelt elk grazes in a mossy forest in Olympic National Park.

In eastern Washington, where there is less rain, common trees include western white pine, ponderosa pine, and western larch. Much of southeastern Washington receives too little rain to support forests. Instead, grasses, sagebrush, and other scattered shrubs grow in the arid ground.

There are hundreds of kinds of wildflowers that add splashes of color to Washington's mountains, seacoasts, and deserts. Common species include tiger lily, alpine yellow monkey-flower, orange agoseris, red columbine, fireweed, bitterroot, and Indian paintbrush. The coast rhododendron is the official state flower.

Grasses, sagebrush, and other shrubs grow in the arid area surrounding Palouse Falls in eastern Washington.

A hoary marmot eats Indian paintbrush flowers at Washington's Mount Rainier National Park.

The largest mammals commonly found living in Washington include deer, elk, coyotes, gray wolves, moose, black bears, cougars, and mountain goats. Smaller animals found scurrying throughout Washington's many habitats include marmots, beavers, muskrats, gophers, raccoons, river otters, opossums, minks, skunks, and squirrels. Rare Cascade red foxes are sometimes spotted on Mount Rainier and Mount Adams. Grizzly bears are sometimes found in the mountains of northern Washington.

Hundreds of species of birds make their home in Washington. They range from waterbirds that live along the Pacific Ocean coast, to species that are found mainly in mountain or desert habitats. Common birds include seagulls, sandpipers, wood ducks, Canada geese, trumpeter swans, black-capped chickadees, downy woodpeckers, red-winged blackbirds, falcons, owls, ruffed grouse, and ravens. The willow goldfinch is Washington's official state bird.

Spotted Owl

Orca

Off Washington's western coast, many marine mammals can be spotted swimming in the Pacific Ocean or the Strait of Juan de Fuca. They include gray and humpback whales, orcas, and harbor seals. Orcas are commonly called killer whales, but they are actually the largest member of the dolphin family.

Common freshwater and saltwater fish found swimming in Washington's lakes, rivers, and ocean waters include rainbow and cutthroat trout, largemouth and smallmouth bass, shad, yellow perch, catfish, sturgeon, walleye, and Pacific salmon. Although born in freshwater, salmon migrate and live most of their lives in the ocean. They then fight their way upstream to their freshwater home to spawn and die.

PLANTS AND ANIMALS

HISTORY

People first came to the Washington area between 10,000 to 12,000 years ago. These Paleo-Indians were the ancestors of today's Native Americans. They were nomads who hunted herds of large animals such as mammoths and bison.

By the time the first Europeans explored Washington, many Native American tribes had established themselves in the area. Some of the largest tribes included the Chinook, Coast Salish, Nez Percé, and Yakima peoples. The Chinook and Coast Salish lived along the Pacific Ocean coast. They fished for salmon in the rivers, and hunted whales in large dugout canoes.

Coast Salish Native Americans in a canoe on Puget Sound.

Captain James Cook, the famous English explorer, is believed to be the first European to trade with Washington's Native Americans in the late 1770s.

In the late 1700s, several Spanish explorers sailed along the Washington coast, searching for riches in the New World. In 1775, Bruno de Heceta claimed the area for Spain. Later treaties allowed other nations to explore.

In 1778, English explorer Captain James Cook also sailed along the Washington coast. He traded with the Native Americans, but rain and fog made mapping too difficult. In 1792, another English explorer, Captain George Vancouver, completed a detailed map of the coast and inland waterways. That same year, Robert Gray, an American sea captain, sailed about 15 miles (24 km) up the Columbia River, naming the river after his ship.

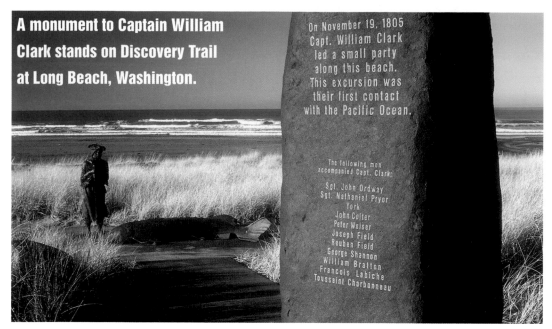

A monument to Captain William Clark stands on Discovery Trail at Long Beach, Washington.

On November 19, 1805 Capt. William Clark led a small party along this beach. This excursion was their first contact with the Pacific Ocean.

The following men accompanied Capt. Clark:

Sgt. John Ordway
Sgt. Nathaniel Pryor
York
John Colter
Peter Weiser
Joseph Field
Reuben Field
George Shannon
William Bratton
Francois Labiche
Toussaint Charbonneau

In 1805, the Lewis and Clark Expedition reached the Washington area. They had traveled overland, all the way across the Great Plains and the Rocky Mountains, from St. Louis, Missouri. On the last part of their journey, they paddled down the Columbia River until reaching the Pacific Ocean.

In the late 1700s and early 1800s, European explorers found that sea otter pelts could be sold for great sums of money in China and Europe. Ships filled with fur trappers and traders from Spain, Great Britain, Russia, France, and the United States descended on the Washington coast. By 1812, the United States dominated the area. Permanent fur-trading posts and villages were built, including a large post near present-day Vancouver, Washington.

Fort Vancouver was built in 1824-1825 as a fur-trading post and supply depot.

Ezra Meeker was a pioneer who followed the Oregon Trail to Washington state in 1858. In the 1900s, he famously made multiple treks back across the country in his ox cart, making speeches to encourage the preservation of the Oregon Trail.

In the 1840s, American settlers began traveling across the continent by way of the Oregon Trail. It was a trail that passed through Kansas, Nebraska, Wyoming, and Idaho before ending in today's Oregon and Washington. Thousands of newcomers arrived, attracted by furs, logging jobs, the promise of gold, and farmland.

In 1848, the United States Congress created Oregon Territory. It included present-day Oregon and Washington, plus parts of Wyoming, Montana, and Idaho. The area proved too large to manage. In 1853, the northern portion became a separate part of the United States. Congress named it Washington Territory.

To encourage growth, Washington officials offered land to settlers. The land was often given away without the knowledge of the Native Americans who lived there. The normally peaceful relationship between the Indians and settlers sometimes turned bloody. The Native Americans fought to keep their ancestral lands. After losing battles with U.S. Army troops, the Indians were forced onto reservations.

A logging train in Washington state. Each railcar holds one to three huge logs.

In the 1880s, the first railroads were built linking Washington with states in the East. The territory's population surged. Forest products and farm goods could be sent by rail, as well as by ships, to faraway markets. Washington's cities grew. On November 11, 1889, Washington became the 42nd state to join the Union.

In 1896, gold was discovered to the north, in Canada's Yukon region. Seattle, with its large port, became a center for gold seekers flocking to Canada. The city grew.

During World War I (1914-1918), Washington's economy boomed. The nation needed the state's vast lumber resources, and the government used Washington's ports to build Navy ships. Also during the war, the Boeing company began manufacturing airplanes in the Seattle area.

The Great Depression struck in 1929. It hit Washington's economy hard, lasting throughout much of the 1930s. Many people lost their jobs, businesses, and homes. One bright spot was the construction of large hydroelectric dams, such as Grand Coulee Dam on the Columbia River. The dams brought electricity to the state's growing industry, and provided irrigation for farming.

World War II B-17 bombers at a Seattle Boeing aircraft factory.

During World War II (1939-1945), Washington's economy improved. Once again, the state's ports were used to construct warships and other vessels. Aircraft manufacturing and nuclear energy projects also helped Washington. The Boeing company produced thousands of military aircraft. Farming and logging also boosted the economy.

After the war, Washington's population grew. The state became a center for many industries. Today, the economy is healthy because so many different kinds of businesses are located there, including companies such as Microsoft, Amazon, and Starbucks.

DID YOU KNOW?

Mount St. Helens — Before The Eruption

After The Eruption

May 18, 1980 Eruption

• The ground shook on May 18, 1980, near beautiful Mount St. Helens, nestled in the Cascade Range in southwestern Washington. The towering volcano had been dormant since 1857, but for several months, steam and small earthquakes had signaled something deep within the Earth was awakening. Suddenly, the top of the mountain blew apart. A plume of hot ash and gasses shot 16 miles (26 km) into the sky. There was so much ash that it blew as far away as Alberta, Canada. An avalanche of lava and mud flowed down the slopes, engulfing everything in its path. Millions of trees were knocked down by the blast. Sadly, 57 people lost their lives. Today, people can visit Mount St. Helens National Volcanic Monument for a glimpse of the volcanic crater, and witness nature as it slowly heals the landscape.

• The Space Needle is one of Seattle's most famous landmarks. The observation tower was built as a centerpiece for the 1962 World's Fair. It was built to show what future skyscrapers might look like in the 2000s. To make the tower as stable as possible, its foundation was a hole dug 30 feet (9 m) deep and 120 feet (37 m) across. It took an entire day for 467 cement trucks to fill the hole. Today, visitors can take a 43-second elevator ride to the saucer-shaped observation deck of the 605-foot (184-m) tower. At the top, there are breathtaking panoramic views of Seattle and the surrounding area, including Puget Sound and the Cascade Range. There is also a rotating restaurant that serves food from the Pacific Northwest.

DID YOU KNOW?

PEOPLE

Chief Seattle (1786-1866) was a leader of the Suquamish and Duwamish Native American tribes, who lived in the Puget Sound region. He was born on Blake Island. While in his 20s, he devised a war strategy that defended his people from an attack by a rival northern tribe. As white settlers came to the Washington area, Chief Seattle

recognized that his people had to adapt to new technology and customs or face extinction. He tried to keep the peace between his people and the settlers, even when Indian land was taken unlawfully. He and his people moved to a reservation, and refused to participate when other tribes went to war against the settlers. Because of his friendship, the city of Seattle was named after him.

Bill Gates (1955-) was born and raised in Seattle. He started writing computer software when he was just 13 years old, which began a lifelong interest in electronics. He went to school at Harvard University, in Cambridge, Massachusetts, but dropped out to start a software company. It eventually became Microsoft Corporation, based in Redmond, Washington. Gates became one of the richest people in the world, thanks to sales of Microsoft Windows, Microsoft Office, Xbox, and many other products. After retiring from the company, Gates started the Bill & Melinda Gates Foundation, which works to reduce disease and poverty around the world. The foundation also promotes education and access to computers.

Bing Crosby (1903-1977) was born in Tacoma, Washington. He became one of the most popular singers and actors in history. His singing style was smooth and relaxed. He was a "crooner," a sentimental, emotional singer backed by an orchestra or band. His biggest hit song was "White Christmas." Crosby also starred in many movies, both comedies and dramas. He won an Academy Award for his role as a priest in the 1944 movie *Going My Way*.

Apolo Ohno (1982-) won many Olympic medals as a short-track speed skater. Born and raised in Seattle, he started competitive swimming and inline skating by age six. By age 12, he became interested in short-track ice skating, where up to six people compete on an oval track about the size of an ice hockey rink. He started winning many championships around the country. He won eight medals, including two gold, at the Winter Olympic Games, more than any other American athlete.

Jimi Hendrix (1942-1970) was a 1960s rock singer, songwriter, and self-taught electric guitar player. He improvised dazzling solos with his mastery of distortion and the wah-wah pedal. Among his many hit songs were "Purple Haze" and "All Along the Watchtower." Sadly, his life was cut short at age 27 by a drug overdose. Hendrix was born in Seattle. He was inducted posthumously into the Rock and Roll Hall of Fame in 1992.

Hilary Swank (1974-) is an Academy-Award winning film and television actress. She was born in Lincoln, Nebraska, but her family moved to Bellingham, in northern Washington, when she was very young. She started acting at an early age. Swank got her first big Hollywood role in 1994, in the movie *The Next Karate Kid*. She went on to win two Academy Awards for her movies *Boys Don't Cry* and *Million Dollar Baby*. Swank is also a successful film producer.

CITIES

Olympia is the capital of Washington. Its population is about 50,302. It is located on the southern end of Puget Sound. Originally the home of Puyallup and Suquamish Native Americans, white settlers arrived in the 1840s. They named the city Olympia because of its view of the Olympic Mountains in the distance. It became the state capital in 1853. Today, Olympia's economy depends on state government, health care, shipping, retail shops, and education. The Evergreen State College enrolls more than 4,500 students, which gives Olympia a laid-back, college-town atmosphere. The heart of downtown is Percival Landing, a waterfront park where people gather for picnics and town celebrations.

Seattle is the largest city in Washington. It is located in the northwestern part of the state, along Puget Sound. Its population is about 684,451. Together with its suburbs and surrounding communities, the entire Seattle metropolitan area is home to more than 3.7 million people. That is more than half of the state's total population. Many large companies operate or have their headquarters in the Seattle area, including Boeing, Starbucks, Microsoft, and Amazon. The University of Washington enrolls more than 45,000 students. The Space Needle is a Seattle landmark, towering 605 feet (184 m) over the skyline. Seattle's waterfront is famous for its fish markets and restaurants. The Seattle Aquarium has six major exhibits featuring marine animals such as harbor seals, giant clams, salmon, and sea stars.

Tacoma is the third-largest city in Washington. Its population is about 207,948. It is located on the southern end of Puget Sound, about 30 miles (48 km) south of Seattle. Settled in the 1850s and 1860s, the city was officially incorporated in 1875. Tacoma is a Native American name for Mount Rainier, the towering peak visible in the southeast. The city is a major shipping center. Large vessels from around the world sail down Puget Sound to Tacoma's deepwater harbor. Once at the city's busy docks, they unload containers of goods, which are whisked away by trucks and trains. Besides shipping, other major employers include manufacturing, health care, and the military. Joint Base Lewis-McChord is a combined U.S. Army-Air Force airlift base just south of the city.

Spokane is Washington's second-largest city. It is home to about 213,272 people. It is located in northeastern Washington, just a few miles from the Idaho border. It is named after the Spokane Native American tribe. The city is home to Whitworth and Gonzaga Universities. The Northwest Museum of Arts & Culture features exhibitions on Native American and regional art and history.

Vancouver is the fourth-largest city in Washington. Its population is about 172,860. It is located in southwestern Washington, along the north bank of the Columbia River. It is across the river from Portland, Oregon. Vancouver had its beginnings as a fur-trading post in 1824. The city was incorporated in 1857. Today, it is a center for high-tech manufacturing, health care, and transportation.

TRANSPORTATION

There are 82,448 miles (132,687 km) of public roadways in Washington. Two major interstate highways cross the state. Interstate I-90 travels east and west, passing through Spokane and ending in Seattle. Interstate I-5 runs north and south. It goes through Vancouver in the south, passes through Tacoma and Seattle, and then heads north until it crosses the border into Canada.

There are 23 railroads in Washington that move freight on 3,192 miles (5,137 km) of track. The most common goods hauled by rail include farm products, lumber, paper and pulp, chemicals, and scrap. Amtrak's Cascades and Coast Starlight lines whisk passengers north and south along the Cascade Range. The Empire Builder runs east and west across the state.

In the Puget Sound area, the Washington State Department of Transportation operates a fleet of ferries. They take people and cars across the waterway. The Washington ferry system is one of the largest in the world.

An Amtrak Cascades train leaves Seattle's King Street Station.

Washington has dozens of ports where goods such as lumber, farm products, aircraft parts, and computers are loaded onto oceangoing ships. The Port of Seattle and the Port of Tacoma are two of the busiest shipping ports in the country.

There are 11 major commercial airports in Washington. The busiest is Seattle-Tacoma International Airport. It serves more than 42 million passengers each year, which makes it the 13th-busiest airport in the nation.

Port of Tacoma

NATURAL
RESOURCES

Washington is one of the top farming states in the nation, thanks to rich soil, a mild climate, and irrigation. The value of the state's agricultural products is more than $10.2 billion. There are about 36,000 farms in Washington, covering 14.7 million acres (5.9 million ha) of land. That is about 35 percent of Washington's total land area.

Top Washington farm products include milk, wheat, potatoes, beef cattle, hay, cherries, grapes, pears, and hops. The state is also a leading producer of cut flowers. Washington is the number-one grower of apples in the United States. Most of the apple orchards are in the east-central part of the state, especially the Wenatchee Valley. The most popular types include red delicious, golden delicious, gala, honeycrisp, and Granny Smith apples.

Gala apples are harvested from an orchard in Finley, Washington. The state is the number-one grower of apples in the United States.

Wild Pacific salmon are caught in Puget Sound and sold to buyers the same day.

Forests cover nearly one-half of Washington. Some of the land is logged, although in recent years strict environmental laws have reduced harvests. Washington exports logs and wood products to other states and countries. It is also a producer of paper.

Along the Pacific Ocean coast, Washington's commercial fishing fleets haul in large catches of halibut, albacore, cod, herring, salmon, and shellfish.

One of Washington's most precious natural resources is the water that flows down waterways such as the Columbia River. Dams along the state's rivers provide needed irrigation for farms, especially in the arid east. The dams also generate electricity for homes and businesses.

NATURAL RESOURCES

INDUSTRY

Washington has many kinds of businesses. This diversity protects the state's economy. If one industry suffers, the economy is held up by the other industries. In recent decades, Washington's economy has shifted from logging and agriculture to manufacturing, especially high-tech products.

There are many manufacturing companies in Washington. In the Seattle area, aircraft and aerospace companies thrive. The Boeing company was founded in Seattle. Today, it operates huge aircraft manufacturing plants in nearby Everett and Renton. The Everett plant, which makes jets such as the Boeing 787 Dreamliner, employs more than 30,000 people. The Renton plant has manufactured more than 11,600 aircraft, which is about 30 percent of all commercial planes flying today.

Boeing 737s are assembled at the company's facility in Renton, Washington.

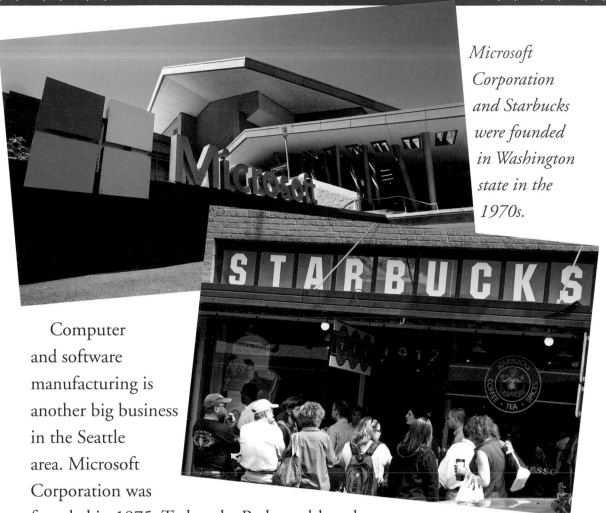

Microsoft Corporation and Starbucks were founded in Washington state in the 1970s.

Computer and software manufacturing is another big business in the Seattle area. Microsoft Corporation was founded in 1975. Today, the Redmond-based company is one of the most important software developers in the world.

Other major products made in Washington include fabricated metal, machinery, and food products. The first Starbucks coffee store opened in Seattle in 1971. The company has expanded so much that today there are more than 24,000 Starbucks stores in 70 countries.

Many Washington workers are employed in the service industry, which includes health care, insurance, advertising, financial services, and marketing. Tourism is very important to Washington's economy. In recent years, visitors have spent almost $18 billion in the state, supporting more than 154,500 jobs.

SPORTS

Washington has several professional major league sports teams. The Seattle Seahawks play in the National Football League (NFL). They have some of the most devoted and noisy fans in the league. The Seahawks won the Super Bowl for the 2013 season. The Seattle Mariners are a Major League Baseball (MLB) team. Nicknamed "the M's," the team has won three American League West Division titles.

The Seattle Sounders FC is a Major League Soccer (MLS) team. The Sounders have won the U.S. Open Cup four times, most recently in 2014. The Seattle Storm plays in the Women's National Basketball Association (WNBA). The team has won two WNBA Finals championships, in 2004 and 2010.

There are many professional minor league sports teams in the state. They play in sports ranging from baseball and ice hockey, to rugby and soccer.

Harry the Husky is the mascot for the University of Washington.

Butch T. Cougar is the mascot for the Washington State Cougars.

Spike the Bulldog is the mascot for the Gonzaga University Bulldogs.

Rudy the Redhawk is the mascot for Seattle University.

Swoop the Eagle is the mascot for Eastern Washington University.

College sports are big in Washington. Some of the most popular teams include the University of Washington Huskies, the Washington State Cougars, the Gonzaga University Bulldogs, the Seattle University Redhawks, and the Eastern Washington University Eagles.

Washington is a paradise for outdoor sports lovers. There are many mountains to climb up or ski down. Campers, hikers, and hunters enjoy trekking through the state's dense forests. There is also great fishing in Washington's many lakes and rivers, and along the Pacific Ocean coast.

SPORTS

ENTERTAINMENT

Washington is well known for its many museums, art galleries, and theater groups. Seattle's EMP Museum is near the historic Space Needle and Seattle Center Monorail. The museum includes many hands-on collections of popular culture, including science fiction television, fantasy literature, and computer gaming.

The Seattle Opera was formed in 1963. Today, it is one of the leading opera companies in the nation. It is famous for staging classical Italian and German operas, as well as popular modern productions. The Seattle Symphony first performed in 1903. It is nationally recognized for its excellence, especially for inspiring young audiences.

Seattle's Monorail enters the 1962 World's Fair site through the EMP Museum. The futuristic museum was designed by architect Frank O. Gehry.

Seattle's Woodland Park Zoo is home to more than 1,000 animals, including birds, mammals, reptiles, amphibians, snails, butterflies, and plants.

There are dozens of world-class museums and art galleries scattered throughout the state. Many feature Native American arts and crafts, including whaling canoes, totem poles, and masks. The Seattle Art Museum contains a collection of more than 24,000 works of fine art, including paintings and sculptures by artists from all over the world.

For nature lovers, Seattle's Woodland Park Zoo is home to more than 1,000 animals. There are 300 species, including endangered tigers and gorillas. Washington has three national parks: Olympic, Mount Rainier, and North Cascades. Olympic National Park includes mountains, rain forests, and more than 70 miles (113 km) of rugged Pacific Ocean coastline to explore.

ENTERTAINMENT

TIMELINE

10,000-8,000 BC—Nomadic Paleo-Indians, the ancestors of today's Native Americans, arrive in the area of present-day Washington.

1700s—Native American tribes established in the Washington area include people from the Chinook, Coast Salish, Nez Percé, and Yakima tribes.

1775—Spanish explorer Bruno de Heceta claims Washington for Spain.

1778—English explorer Captain James Cook sails along the Washington coast.

1792—English explorer Captain George Vancouver explores and maps the area's coast and waterways.

1805—The Lewis and Clark Expedition reaches the Washington area.

1824—Hudson's Bay Company establishes Fort Vancouver.

1848—Oregon Territory is formed, which includes most of present-day Washington.

1853—Washington Territory is formed, breaking off from Oregon Territory.

1889—Washington becomes the 42nd state.

1929—The Great Depression begins. Washington's economy is hit hard.

1941-1945—America's involvement in World War II brings better economic times to the state.

1980—Mount St. Helens erupts on the morning of May 18, killing 57 people and thousands of plants and animals.

2010—The Seattle Storm wins the Women's National Basketball Association Finals championship.

2014—The Seattle Seahawks win the Super Bowl for the 2013 season. The Seattle Sounders FC win the U.S. Open Cup for the 4th time.

2016—The University of Washington Huskies women's golf team wins the NCAA National Championship.

GLOSSARY

DECIDUOUS

A tree or other plant that sheds its leaves each autumn.

FUR TRAPPER

A person who catches animals for their soft, thick coats of hair, which are later made into clothing such as coats or hats.

GLACIER

Often called rivers of ice, glaciers are made of thick sheets of compacted snow. They are often formed in mountainous areas, where near-constant freezing conditions cause centuries of snow to accumulate, compact, and turn to ice. The ice slowly creeps downhill, scouring and smoothing the landscape underneath.

GREAT DEPRESSION

A time in American history beginning in 1929 and lasting for several years when many businesses failed and millions of people lost their jobs. The Great Depression hit Washington very hard.

HYDROELECTRIC POWER

When rivers are dammed, a controlled flow of water runs turbines, which drive generators that create electricity.

LEWIS AND CLARK EXPEDITION

An exploration of the American West, led by Meriwether Lewis and William Clark, from 1804-1806.

PELT

The skin of an animal, with the fur still attached. People in the 1700s and 1800s paid large sums of money for animal pelts, such as beavers and sea otters, to make hats and other items of clothing.

PLATEAU

A large area of land that is mainly flat but much higher than the land that neighbors it.

POSTHUMOUS

An award or honor given after the death of the person receiving it.

SOUND

A large waterway or ocean inlet.

WAH-WAH PEDAL

A guitar effects pedal that resembles a car's gas pedal. It lets a musician adjust a guitar's sound by rocking his or her foot back and forth. It alters the sound from the guitar, making the musical note sound like a human voice saying the word "wah."

WORLD WAR I

A war that was fought in Europe from 1914 to 1918, involving countries around the world. The United States entered the war in April 1917.

WORLD WAR II

A conflict that was fought from 1939 to 1945, involving countries around the world. The United States entered the war after Japan bombed the American naval base at Pearl Harbor, in Oahu, Hawaii, on December 7, 1941.

INDEX